P9-DGE-231

make-up

Style Me Vintage

Katie Reynolds has been a hair and make-up artist for over 12 years, working in film, TV, music, commercials and fashion, with a celebrity client list. She founded The Powderpuff Girls in 2005 – a unique team of beauty professionals who provide a pampering service for events and parties. The girls also work at The Powder Room, a vintage-style beauty parlour open for everyone to come and experience their expertise! www.thepowderpuffgirls.com

Katie Reynolds

tyle Me Vintage

Easy step-by-step techniques for creating classic looks

make-up

First published in the United Kingdom in 2011 by
PAVILION BOOKS
10 Southcombe Street, London W14 0RA
An imprint of Anova Books Company Ltd

Text © Katie Reynolds, 2011
Design and layout © Anova Books, 2011
Photography © Anova Books, 2011,
except those images listed in Acknowledgements p.112

The moral right of the author has been asserted.

All rights reserved. No part of this publication may be reproduced, stored in a retrieval system, or transmitted in any form or by any means electronic, mechanical, photocopying, recording or otherwise, without the prior written permission of the copyright owner.

Commissioning editor: Nina Sharman
Designer: Georgina Hewitt
Copy editor: Julia Halford
Photographer: Christina Wilson
Hair and make-up: Katie Reynolds
Hair and make-up assistant: Bethany Swan
Manicures: Bethany Swan and Dominika Kasperowicz
Clothing stylist: Heather MacVean
Models: Hannah Maxwell, Leah Ward, Sophia St Villier, Jasmin Paynter, Miss Betsy Rose, Alex Grindley, Zara Sparkes, Fifi Fatale, Maia Smillie

ISBN: 9781862059184

A CIP catalogue record for this book is available from the British Library.

10 9 8 7 6 5 4 3

Colour reproduction by Rival Colour Ltd., UK
Printed and bound by Toppan Lee-Fung Printing Ltd, China

www.anovabooks.com

Contents

Introduction

It's easy to bring a touch of old-fashioned glamour back into our lives – a little decadent time spent on ourselves is an experience that everyone deserves. Looking radiant and fabulous need not be a chore, but a joy!

I aspire to the poised and ladylike allure of past decades, but that is not to say we all have to wear stockings and red lipstick (although highly recommended) – the same principles can be applied to any era. Making yourself look good makes you feel good, and make-up is one of life's little luxuries that we can always afford. The Lipstick Effect – the theory that women buy more cosmetics during hard times to cheer themselves up instead of more expensive luxury items – can be seen as far back as The Great Depression of the 1930s.

At The Powder Room, we try to bring this experience to all you deserving glamourettes. But for those we can't reach, I have put together a 'how to' guide to achieving our favourite retro looks at home. Goddess Dita Von Teese once replied in an interview, when asked what she liked least about herself, that she would never draw attention to her flaws. This is a superb rule for life, as people generally don't notice flaws unless they are pointed out. In the same way, this book is all about accentuating your best features and not worrying about flaws!

'It's your duty to be beautiful!'

Katie
x

Tips and Tools

Here are a few useful tips that we think will help you to recreate the glamour of the past, and the essential items you'll need to achieve it.

- A good skincare routine is the best place to start. Always cleanse, tone and moisturise, and NEVER go to sleep in your makeup!

- Two items you really can't skimp on are a good foundation and primer. Primer will make your foundation go on more smoothly and will help fix it all day. Make sure you get the right shade for your skin tone and that, when applied, your face looks the same colour as your neck! If you can create the best possible blank canvas, the rest of your make-up will look divine.

- If you want heavier eye make-up with dark eyeshadows, a good tip is to apply your foundation *after* finishing your eyes, as some eyeshadows can drop onto your foundation during application, spoiling all your good work.

- When doing any part of your make-up, wipe off any excess product on your brush onto the back of your hand first – it is much better to start light and build up.

- When choosing red lipsticks… generally, blue-reds suit fair, pink-toned skin, and orange-reds suit dark, yellow-toned skin. But there are exceptions to every rule, so try a few and choose what makes you feel the most fabulous.

- Finally, well-groomed eyebrows are a must. Most brows will need a little help with tweezers and make-up. It's worth it – your make-up simply doesn't look finished without!

Handy Tools

wedge sponges (non-latex)

cotton buds

essential brushes: powder, blusher,
defining brush, eyeshadow brush,
socket brush, blending brush, eyeliner brush,
eyebrow brush, retractable lip brush
for your handbag

blotting papers

false eyelashes

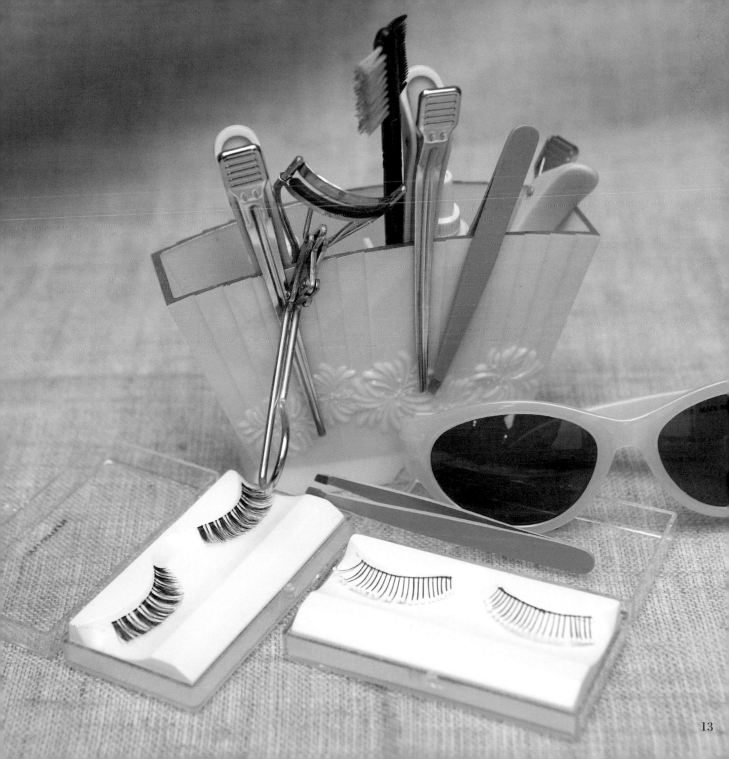

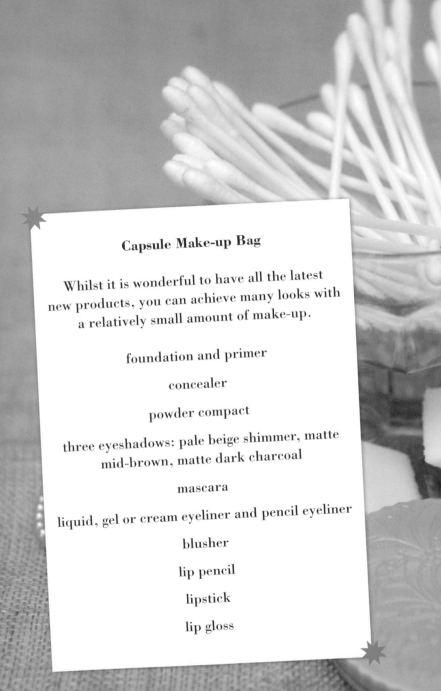

Capsule Make-up Bag

Whilst it is wonderful to have all the latest new products, you can achieve many looks with a relatively small amount of make-up.

foundation and primer

concealer

powder compact

three eyeshadows: pale beige shimmer, matte mid-brown, matte dark charcoal

mascara

liquid, gel or cream eyeliner and pencil eyeliner

blusher

lip pencil

lipstick

lip gloss

The following pages will show you how to recreate some iconic looks from past decades that we think are still very popular and wearable today, and can be brought up to date with a few little changes here and there. They are also the basis for many modern adaptations, so once you have mastered these simple techniques you will be a dab hand at a great many others, too!

The Looks

Twenties...
Then and Now

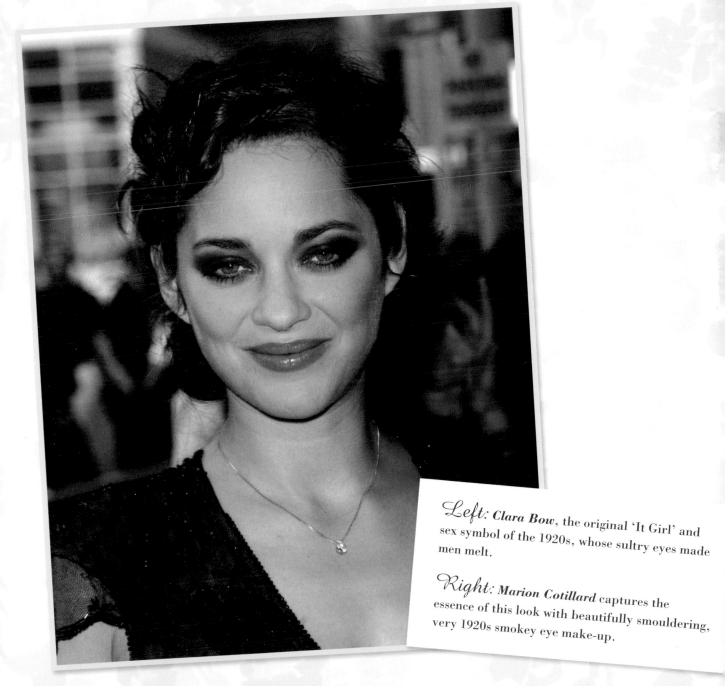

Left: **Clara Bow**, the original 'It Girl' and sex symbol of the 1920s, whose sultry eyes made men melt.

Right: **Marion Cotillard** captures the essence of this look with beautifully smouldering, very 1920s smokey eye make-up.

1920s
Clara Bow

After the Edwardian era, with its soft, delicate make-up and very long hair, and World War I, when make-up was scarce, the 1920s was a stark contrast. Particularly during the 'Roaring Twenties' – between 1925 and 1929 – dressing up, dancing and partying was a huge part of life. Icons of this period included Clara Bow, Louise Brooks and Josephine Baker – huge stars of their day, with their short bobbed haircuts and strikingly heavily made-up looks. The classic look of the flapper girls of the jazz clubs was dark, smoky kohl-rimmed eyes; long, dark eyebrows; and small, very dark-red rosebud lips.

Step 1

Start with a blank canvas – your face should be perfectly primed and ready for foundation. Apply foundation with a brush, sponge or simply fingers! Make sure you blend well and have no streaks or edges – a wedge sponge is good for this. (When doing smoky eyes, you may want to apply foundation after step 6.) Prime the eyes, and cover with a light eye concealer – some products do both these jobs in one. Lightly powder all over.

Step 2

With a very soft black or grey kohl eye pencil, line your eyes all the way around and smudge and soften the edges. You can also line the inside of the lower lid.

Step 3

Take your eyeshadow brush and coat it with your charcoal eyeshadow; gently dab off any excess on the back of your hand. Begin sparingly and, in very small circular movements, start at the outer edge of the lid and socket, and gradually blend towards the inner corner.

Step 4

Eyebrows were quite thin and dark, long and angled down. If you wish, you can just define them well with a small angled brush and a complimentary eyeshadow or a matte pencil.

You can repeat Step 3 until you get the required density. Much better to build up gradually. Use your blending brush to make sure you don't have any hard edges.

Step 5

Apply lashings of mascara to the top and bottom eyelashes.

Step 6

Apply a subtle dusting of a peachy blusher to the apples of the cheeks (find these by smiling – the apples are the parts of your cheek that rise up into a round shape).

Step 7

Line lips with pencil and apply dark red lipstick to create a well-defined small rosebud, to complete the starlet look. If you have a wider mouth you can still achieve this look, just don't take your lip line right to the corners. A neutral lip colour or gloss also suits this look and brings it more up to date.

Thirties...
Then and Now

Left: *Marlene Dietrich.* With her cool, mysterious and disarming beauty, even wearing masculine clothing didn't detract from her allure.

Right: *Christina Aguilera* often opts for vintage glamour for her look, and this look has a thoroughly 1930s feel.

1930s
Marlene Dietrich

The era of the silver-screen goddess, 1930s' style was very different to that of the heavy make-up and short flapper dresses of the 1920s. This was the era of the long cream silk evening gown, cut on the bias to accentuate all those curves, rather than the flattened busts of the twenties! Goddesses of the day included Marlene Dietrich, Jean Harlow and Greta Garbo, who all embodied the perfect glamour of the decade. Hair was slightly longer and softly waved, eyes were glossy in golds and champagnes to compliment those evening dresses, eyebrows were pencil-thin, long and highly arched, and lips were a lighter, softer red with a curved cupid's bow.

Step 1

Start with a blank canvas (perfectly primed), and apply your foundation. Prime the eyes and cover with a light eye concealer (some products do both these jobs in one). Apply light powder all over.

Step 2

Take your eyeshadow brush and coat it with a soft gold or champagne colour and sweep across the entire eyelid and browbone. Repeat on the other side. This should be shimmery.

Step 3

Take your socket brush and, with a very subtle neutral stone or light brown, shade in the socket. If you tilt your head down slightly you will find it easier to find the correct place to shade. You want to create a sleepy hooded eye, so don't blend too far up to the browbone.

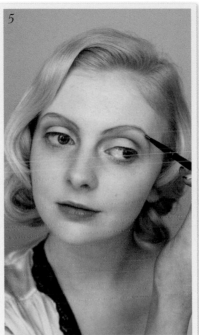

Step 4

Take your eyeliner brush and apply a thin line across the top lashes, not too extended.

Step 5

Eyebrows were extremely pencil-thin, but don't feel you need to pluck them all away! You can just define them well with a small angled brush and a complementary eyeshadow or a pencil.

Step 6

Apply lashings of mascara or, even better, a really fine, feathery set of false eyelashes (see page 100).

To achieve shiny, glossy lids, people sometimes used to apply Vaseline over their eyeshadow.

Step 7

Apply a very subtle dusting of a pale peachy blusher to the apples of the cheeks (see page 24), and more blusher evenly blended across the cheekbone. If you don't have the highly sculpted cheekbones of Marlene Dietrich, you can fake it by shading a little under your cheekbone with a darker, beigey blusher – you can find where to apply it by sucking in your cheeks!

Step 8

Finally, for an authentic look, add a soft shiny red lipstick to fully lined lips with rounded cupid's bow. Marlene would pencil outside her natural lip line to create this.

Forties...
Then and Now

Left: *Rita Hayworth* epitomised Hollywood glamour, a look that women the world over wanted.

Right: *Paloma Faith* perfectly captures the essence of the 1940s, but with her own quirky take on this glamorous look.

1940s
Rita Hayworth

Make-up in the 1940s was all about the lipstick – and matte red was the look. Even land girls wouldn't be seen without it! During World War II, make-up was in short supply so women became very inventive – using boot polish for mascara, for example! Women in the 1940s aspired to the Hollywood version, typified by Rita Hayworth, and although few could achieve it in such tough times, they still made the effort to be glamorous!

Step 1

As always, start with perfectly primed skin and apply your foundation and powder well – matte was the order of the day. Prime eyes, too, and use a light concealer.

Step 2

With your eyeshadow brush, apply a neutral beige colour to the whole eyelid.

Step 3

Take your socket brush and, with a very subtle neutral stone or light brown, shade in the socket. If you tilt your head down slightly you will find it easier to find the correct place to shade. You want it barely there for a daytime look, but you can go slightly darker for evening looks.

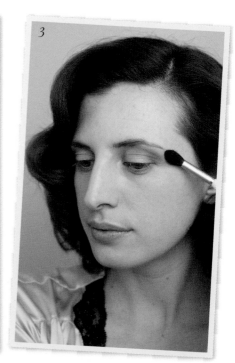

Step 4

Take a good liquid eyeliner and apply a very thin line along the eyelashes of your upper lid, from the inner towards the outer corner, and extend it slightly.

Step 5

Use an angled brush to define your eyebrows and gently accentuate the arch, in a complementary or slightly darker colour.

Step 6

Use lashings of mascara – for an authentic look, just apply to the upper lashes. For Hollywood glamour, false eyelashes are essential (see page 100).

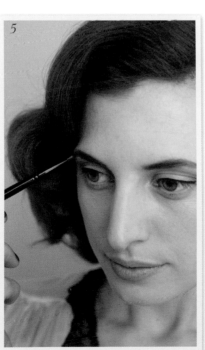

Step 7

Rouge was popular in the 1930s, so a light dusting of rosy pink to the apples will compliment this look.

Step 8

Lips need to be perfectly lined with a good red pencil that matches your lipstick, and the lipstick needs to be a very matte pillar-box red. Blot well.

Fifties ...
Then and Now

Left: **Marilyn Monroe,** with her voluptuous curves, was always the perfect sex symbol throughout the 1950s, whether in an evening dress or jeans and a sweater.

Right: **Scarlett Johansson** epitomises a modern-day 1950s' pin-up, and can carry off all of Marilyn's looks to perfection.

43

1950s
Marilyn Monroe

The 1950s saw much more colour in both make-up and fashion – in fact, it was quite the done thing to match your eyeshadow to your handbag! Blues and greens or pinks and violets were popular for eyes, and corals and pinks for lips. Eyebrows were more defined and angled sharply, and tans were in fashion – fake or otherwise! Blondes were still favoured, and what better bombshell to emulate than Marilyn Monroe? A perfect cross between girl next door and sex kitten.

Step 1

As always, start with perfectly primed skin and apply your foundation. A more tanned complexion was fashionable and not too matte – so keep a little natural shine.

Step 2

With your eyeshadow brush, cover the whole eyelid up to the brow with a light, shimmery golden champagne colour.

Step 3

Take your socket brush and, in round circular movements, make a really natural socket shading with a taupe colour.

Step 4

Take your eyeshadow brush again and, with a soft coral/pink (or a blue or green), go over the eyelid from the outer corner fading to the inner corner.

Step 5

With a fine eyeliner brush, using a brown or black, take a fine line across the top lid along the lashes: tapering narrowest at the inner corner, getting thicker to the outer corner, and slightly elongate the line and flick up the end a little into a point. A good tip is to lift your chin while still looking in the mirror – this will enable you to apply the line with your eye still open, which will be much smoother than if you close one eye.

Step 6

With your angled brush, using a matte colour to compliment your eyebrows, enhance your eyebrows with short brush strokes into a sharp angle – thicker at the inner end and tapering off to a point at the outer end.

Step 7

Mascara the top lashes thickly, and the bottom ones just a little.

Step 8

Use a warm corally pink for your blusher, in round movements over the apples (see page 24), and a little up the cheekbones.

Step 9

Take a pinky red or corally red lip pencil and line your lips. They should be more rounded than a 1940s' cupid's bow but not as rounded as the 1930s' shape. Fill in with a matching lipstick – not too matte, more glossy was the look.

For a really authentic Marilyn look, you could add a beauty spot just outside your smile line, and white eye pencil inside the lower eyelid.

1960s

Audrey Hepburn

The effortlessly chic Audrey Hepburn was a classic style icon of the 1950s and 1960s. However, it was her early 1960s *Breakfast at Tiffany's* look, as Holly Golightly, that went on to inspire styles that everyone wanted to emulate. Less colour, more natural lips, heavier eye make-up, and lashings of eyeliner!

Step 1

With perfectly primed skin, apply your foundation and powder. You can even dab a little foundation on your lips with a sponge, as very nude lips were part of the look. Prime the eyes as well, and use a light concealer. Lightly powder all over the face and eyes.

Step 2

With your eyeshadow brush, apply a pale taupe colour to the whole eyelid and browbone.

Step 3

Take your socket brush, and with a very dark grey or black eyeshadow shade in the socket. If you tilt your head down slightly you will find it easier to find the correct place to shade.

Step 4

Take a good liquid, gel or cream eyeliner, and with a fine-pointed brush, apply a line along the eyelashes of your upper lid from the inner to the outer corner. You can go quite thick with this, building up gradually, but make sure it is thinner at the inner corner and goes to a point at the other end – you want the classic flick at the outer corners (see page 98). As before, if you lift your chin so that you are looking down into a mirror with both eyes just barely open, your eyelids won't screw up and you will find it easier to get a smooth line.

Step 5

Use an angled brush to define your eyebrows in a slightly darker colour. Audrey Hepburn-style eyebrows were very defined, thickened above the brow and very angled.

Step 6

Use plenty of mascara or, even better, false eyelashes (see page 100).

Step 7

You want barely there blusher in a pale colour – peaches and apricots work well. A little on the apples (see page 24) and up along the top of the cheekbone.

Step 8

Use a very natural pinkish lip colour – not too glossy but not matte.

Left: **Audrey Hepburn** – elegance personified, her looks were copied throughout the 1950s.

Below: **Natalie Portman** has the beautiful delicate features that give her the same classic Audrey look.

Audrey
Inspiration

Sixties...
Then and Now

Left: **Twiggy's** look was a complete revolution and inspired a whole generation.

Right: **Carey Mulligan** captures a similar elfin androgyny with a more modern and less theatrical 1960s-style make-up – very pared-down, but still maintaining strong eyes.

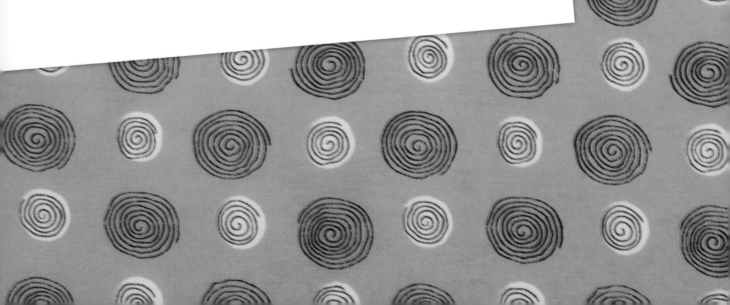

1960s
Twiggy

A key 1960s look was that of the child-like innocence epitomised by Twiggy. Essential elements were: mini skirts and flat shoes, short neat little bobs, perfect natural complexion, nude glossy lips, and round doll-like eyes with huge eyelashes top and bottom. Although colours and flowers featured heavily towards the end of the sixties, it is the combination of monochrome clothing and heavily made-up eyes that truly embodies the 'Swinging Sixties'.

Step 1

Start with perfectly primed skin. Apply your foundation very lightly – keeping it natural. If you have freckles, embrace them and don't cover them up! Prime eyes, too, and use a light concealer. Lightly powder all over face and eyes.

Step 2

With your eyeshadow brush, apply any pastel colour or even white to the whole eyelid.

Step 3

Take your socket brush and, with a very dark grey or black eyeshadow, shade in the socket. If you tilt your head down slightly, you will find it easier to find the correct place to shade. You can blend this a little, but a really defined and arched socket line was very sixties. You can even use an eyeliner pencil if you want a really authentic look.

Step 4

Take a good liquid, gel or cream eyeliner, and with a fine-pointed brush, apply a line along the eyelashes of your upper lid from the inner to the outer corner. You can build this up gradually, but make sure it is thinner at the inner corner and goes to a point at the other end. Add the classic flick (see page 98) at the outer corners, but make it longer, much thicker and more pronounced for this look.

Step 5

For an authentic Twiggy, you will want to paint on a few lower lashes at the outer corner of the lower lid. Be sure to taper them off to a point and curve them slightly.

Step 6

Use an angled brush to define your eyebrows, but keep them very natural.

Step 7

Lashings of mascara, and false eyelashes (see page 100) are an absolute must – the thicker the better! Twiggy was famous for wearing three pairs!

Step 8

You want barely there blusher in a pale colour. Apply a little on the apples (see page 24) and carry on up along the top of the cheekbone slightly. This look was all about the eyes, so everything else was pared right down.

9

Step 9

Lips should be nude – just a very natural gloss. You could even use foundation instead of lipstick to achieve a 1960s' look.

Seventies...
Then and Now

Left: *Farrah Fawcett* is an all-American picture of health with her flowing hair and sunkissed make-up.

Right: Blonde and beautiful, *Kate Hudson* also always looks bronzed, dewy and healthy.

1970s
Farrah Fawcett

The 1970s was all about looking naturally fit, glowing and healthy, à la Charlie's Angels. The perfectly tanned, toned and highlighted Farrah Fawcett was the ultimate icon of the era, with her bronzed make-up, lots of eye shadow and healthy shiny lips. But some people also loved a good splash of Studio 54 glitz and glamour for the evenings, with plenty of glitter and gloss!

Step 1

As always, start with perfectly primed skin and apply your foundation. A tanned-looking complexion is what's needed here, with a little natural shine. Powder with a slightly bronzed powder or one that has some shimmer, to add to the glowing, healthy tanned look.

Step 2

With your eyeshadow brush, use a warm golden brown or an olive green and lightly take it over the whole eyelid up to the crease.

Step 3

Take your socket brush, and with a darker bronzy brown, work in small circular movements from the outer edge of the socket line and fade out to the centre.

Step 4

With your defining brush, take a dark brown or black eyeshadow; start at the outer edge of your eye and work along the top lashes, tapering and fading off just past the centre. You want this to look like a softer, more smudgy eyeline. Repeat along the lower lash line, again tapering and fading off just past the centre.

Step 5

Apply plenty of thick mascara, and define eyebrows with a natural brown eyeshadow or pencil.

Step 6

For blusher, use an orangey brick colour or bronzer; take along the cheekbones, not onto the apples.

Step 7

Lips should be glossy and shiny.

Eighties...
Then and Now

Left: *Siouxie Sioux*, the unique face of rock and punk in the 1970s and 80s, had such artistic flair with her make-up.

Right: *Jessie J* is also very creative with her make-up. This is still quite a striking rock chick look, but more wearable.

1980s
Siouxie Sioux

Punk was a huge scene in the 1970s and early 1980s, with Siouxie Sioux being someone you could aspire to look like or just dip into now and again as part of your own mini-rebellion. This is quite a dramatic look and not for the faint-hearted! The overall effect is very sharp and angular. You can, of course, pare this right down; leaving out her trademark eyebrows and shortening the eyelines would make it much more wearable. The eyeliner could be much finer, and you don't have to have such a pale face!

Step 1

Start with perfectly primed skin and apply your foundation and powder well (this was a matte look). Keep your complexion pale, but not paler than your neck. Prime eyes, too, and use a light concealer. As this look has lots of dark, heavy eyeshadow, you may want to apply your foundation later (after step 3).

Step 2

Take your eyeshadow brush and load it up with a light, matte, neutral colour and take this all over the lid up to the brow. This is just to help you blend later.

Step 3

Apply a black eyeshadow all over the eyelid and into the socket line, building up the intensity as you go but taking care not to go into the inner hollow against the nose. Take your blending brush and blend up towards the browbone and out towards the temples, making sure you have no edges.

Step 4

With your eyeliner brush, load up with black liquid, gel or cream eyeliner and, as with the 1960s, take it along the lash line of the top lid from inner corner to outer. For authenticity, you can extend this right down to the inner corner and onto the nose, and also elongate it at the outer corner towards the temples. Again, build up the thickness gradually.

Step 5

With the same eyeliner brush, follow the lower lash line from inner to outer (this line is not as thick as the top line). Extend the line on to the nose, parallel with the upper line, leaving a gap in between. Join up with the top line at the outer corner. Fill in the gap at the inner corner with a white pencil.

Step 6

Apply plenty of thick mascara.

Step 7

With the black eyeshadow, take your angled brush and start to work into the eyebrows. The shape is not a natural one – it is very thick and straight-edged, tapering down along the nose and elongated outwards towards the temple.

Step 8

No blusher is needed for this look – just a little shading with a brown eyeshadow to enhance the cheekbones (see page 32).

Step 9

Lips had a very pointed cupid's bow, and were in a very dark glossy red.

1980s
Madonna

The 1980s was a 'more is more' era. Whether it was money, power or hair and make-up, everything was big! Lots of eye make-up, coloured mascara, strong blusher and frosted, metallic lip shades. What with so much power-dressing, inspired by films like *Working Girl*, and the rich and immaculately polished looks of 'Dynasty' and 'Dallas', it was no wonder that the devil-may-care Madonna was a breath of fresh air! The remnants of Punk became softer, merging into the pop scene – and the looks of *Desperately Seeking Susan* and 'Like a Virgin' were copied everywhere.

Step 1

Start with perfectly primed skin, and apply a good coverage foundation (use concealer and powder well). This wasn't a 'natural' look.

Step 2

Take a good orangey eyeshadow, and lightly dust it all over the eyelid. Concentrate the colour to the outer corner of the eyelid and into the socket, fading out slightly towards the inner corner and brow (or use a yellowy gold in the inner corner).

Step 3

With a darker eyeshadow, take a little of this along the top lashes – it should be thicker at the outer corner, fading out after the centre. Repeat along the bottom lashes.

Step 4

You can intensify this with a pencil to get a stronger look, provided you have a smudger, so you can blend it out.

Step 5

Apply plenty of mascara. Lots of mascara was fashionable in the 1980s.

Step 6

Eyebrows were 'natural' and brushed upwards. Don't feel you have to grow yours for this look, just give them a good brush upwards and you will have an eighties feel!

Step 7

Use an orangey brick colour blusher, and apply it right along the edge of the cheekbone and into the hollow underneath, to give a bit of shading.

Step 8

Lipsticks were generally very metallic and shimmery in the 1980s but, for this look, Madonna wore an orangey red lipstick.

You could also add Madonna's trademark beauty spot on the upper lip!

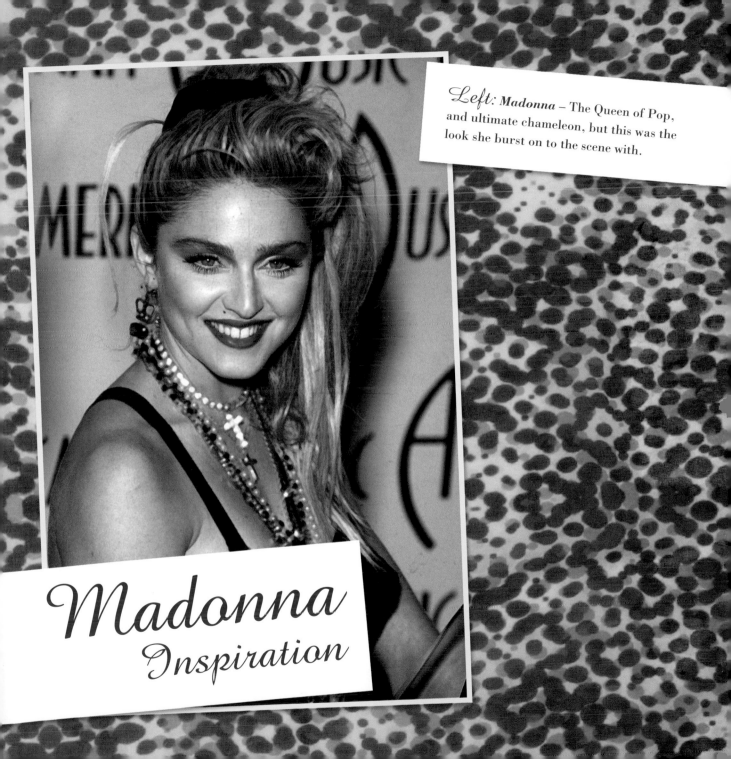

Left: **Madonna** – The Queen of Pop, and ultimate chameleon, but this was the look she burst on to the scene with.

Madonna
Inspiration

Extras

Fabulous Flicks

One thing that people often find difficult to do themselves is applying liquid eyeliner, especially with a vintage-style flick-up at the ends. Here are a few tips that will help you, but practise makes perfect! You will need a compact mirror so you can get up close, and it is usually much easier to use a really good eyeliner brush rather than the applicator that comes with the product. You may also find a cream or gel eyeliner easier to use than a liquid, as it is a bit easier to control.

1. Dip your brush into your chosen eyeliner, and make sure it is well coated. Wipe off the excess on the back of your hand, spinning the brush so as to make it into a good point.
2. Take your compact mirror and hold it slightly lower down. Raise your chin so your eyes are almost closed – this will allow you to keep both eyes open. If you close one eye, it tends to screw up slightly and you won't get a smooth line.
3. If you don't feel confident to do a line in one sweep, start in the middle and take the line out to the outer corner. You can keep going over this, each time edging gradually further towards the inner corner.
4. Try not to pull your eyelid taut, as this can distort the line. You want to keep your eyelid in as natural a position as possible so you can see exactly where to put the line.
5. You want your line to finely taper off at the inner corner and get thicker towards the outer corner, tapering off upwards into a flick.
6. Make sure the flick is a smooth curve rather than a tick. A good rule of thumb is to follow the curve of your lower lid as if you were extending that curve.

Luscious Lashes

False eyelashes have had something of a resurgence in recent years, and can really enhance your make-up. These days, you can have semi-permanent individual lashes attached to your own lashes for a really natural look, which is hard to detect even close up. But this is time-consuming and expensive, and you can't do this yourself at home – so here are some tips for you to try yourself.

Full-strip lashes

These give the most dramatic effect, although you can get some quite thin and natural strips. They usually come with their own glue, but if they don't you will need to get a latex-based eyelash glue.

1. Before you glue the lashes on, measure them for size along your own lashes. The longest lashes are for the outside edge of your eye. If they are too wide, cut them down lash by lash from the outside edge until they are the right width for you.
2. Squeeze out some of the glue on to the back of your hand; don't squeeze directly on to the lashes, and never directly on to your eyelid.
3. Run the lashes through the glue so that there is an even amount of glue all along the lash.
4. Blow onto the glue on the lashes, or leave them for several seconds. This allows the glue to start to set and become more tacky, which will make it much easier and quicker to fix them in place.
5. Once tacky, close one eye without screwing it up (raising your eyebrows helps to keep the skin smooth) and place the lashes outer-edge first as close to your own lashes as possible. Gently press into place with your fingertips or a cotton bud, paying particular attention to the corners. (Some people will use tweezers at this point but, if you do, please make sure you are not in danger of your hand slipping or anyone jogging you. Sharp, pointy things near the eye is never a good thing!)
6. Repeat on the other side, and then blend any edges with some liquid eyeliner.

Half-strip Lashes

You can buy half-length strip lashes or you can cut the full length ones in half. This look really suits and enhances a 1950s' flicked eyeline. Apply half-strip lashes in the same way as the full strip, fixing to the outer corner first.

Individual Lashes

You can buy either single lashes or lashes in a group of three or more, fanning out from a single point. Both come in different lengths and look very natural. This process is quite fiddly to do, so you may want a friend to help you.

1. You will probably only want to apply four or five individual lashes to each eye, so pick them out and line them up for each eye before you start. You want the longest ones for the outer corners, getting shorter as you move along the lash line towards the centre. You may only want them to go as far as the centre, as they look more obvious towards the inner corner.
2. Squeeze the glue on to the back of your hand as before and, taking the longest lash, dip the bulb into the glue and allow it to dry slightly.
3. Place the lash right into the lash line at the outer corner.
4. Repeat along the lash line, spacing well. Make sure you put them in at the same angle as your natural lashes, otherwise they could all stick out at different angles – looking rather too spidery!

Beautiful Brows

Because eyebrows were so defining of an era – from the pencil-thin brows of the 1930s to the natural, bushy brushed-up eyebrows of the 1980s – it is rather too drastic to actually change them for a particular make-up look. Retro looks are all about a nod towards an era rather than slavishly following a look. Keeping them tidy and groomed will complete any look perfectly. There are plenty of brow bars these days where you can get them professionally threaded or waxed, but it's so simple to just pluck them yourself at home.

You will need a really good pair of tweezers – quality really does matter in this instance. Slant-edged are easiest to use and they need to be sharp, but not so sharp as to cut the hairs. To ensure your tweezers keep a good grip on the hairs, regularly wipe the tips. Please try to avoid over-plucking – it can take an age for brows to grow back!

1. Make sure that you're near a window – daylight is quite unforgiving and will show up everything! Magnifying mirrors can really help, as you can see each hair very clearly, but keep checking the entire look in a standard mirror.
2. The space between your brows should not be too wide. To find where your brow should start, take a make-up brush and hold it parallel to the side of your nose. Where the brush meets your brow is where your brow should begin. You can get a good idea of where to end the length of your brow by extending the brush diagonally from your nostril to the outside edge of your eye.
3. Most brows look best with a slight arch. To know where to make this, hold the brush parallel to the outside edge of the iris to see where the highest part of the arch should be.
4. Proceed with caution and stop every few hairs to look at the whole shape. Pluck hairs one at a time, and in the direction they grow. You may find it easier and less painful if you hold the skin taut.
5. When you have achieved your desired shape, brush through your brows. You can apply something soothing like a toner to calm any redness and help close the pores.
6. If your brows are sparse or have gaps, you can fill them in by brushing a matte brown eyeshadow using an angled brush or an eyeliner pencil. Use short strokes in the direction of the hairs to make them look as if they are real hairs.
7. For unruly, wayward eyebrows, a dab of gel smoothed through or a little hairspray sprayed onto a brow brush and brushed through will help them stay put!

Marvellous Manicures

A good manicure will finish off your look perfectly, so taking care of your hands and nails is an important part of your beauty routine. A really cheap and easy way to get smooth hands is to rub them with a mixture of almond oil and sugar and then rinse in warm water; this exfoliates and moisturises them at the same time. If your cuticles need work, soak your hands in warm water first for at least five minutes, to soften the cuticles. Massage in some cuticle oil, and push the cuticles back gently using a soft rubber hoof stick rather than an orange stick – this will avoid causing any damage to the cuticle. This is much better for your cuticles than than trimming or cutting them.

Now your hands are prepped, you will need the following: nail polish remover, cotton wool pads, cotton buds, nail file (not metal), nail buffer, base coat, colour and top coat.

1. Firstly, remove any old nail polish. Soak a cotton pad in nail polish remover; press onto nail and hold for several seconds, and then gently rub away from the skin around the nail until all traces of the old nail polish have been removed.
2. Take your nail file and file nails to the desired shape; oval shapes tend to suit most people. File in one direction only using the coarse side of the emery board to shorten and shape the nail, and then smooth the edge with the finer side.
3. If your nails have ridges or are uneven, you can smooth them with a nail buffer, starting with the roughest side and ending with the smoothest side.
4. Use a cotton wool pad with some nail polish to wipe over the nails to get rid of any dust from filing and buffing, or any oil that would prevent the nail polish 'sticking' correctly.
5. Always use a base coat – it provides a smooth surface for polish and prevents nail polish from staining the nails. Apply one coat: one stroke of polish down the middle, then one on either side of the nail. Try not to keep going over each stroke.
6. Apply two coats of your colour in the same way, taking care not to stray onto the cuticle or skin around the nail.
7. Top coats add shine and help your manicure last longer without chipping, especially if you re-apply everyday. Apply one coat in the same manner.
8. You can correct any straying bits of nail polish around your nails or cuticles with a cotton bud dipped in to nail polish remover, or better still there are some great corrector pens on the market!

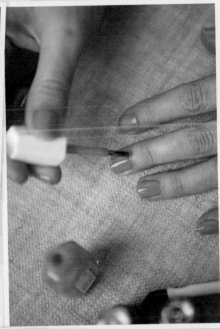

There are quick-dry sprays and polish that will help your nails dry quickly (touch dry in about five minutes). It's best, however, to be careful not to knock them for at least half an hour to ensure that they are completely dry.

1940s-style Manicure

Fashions in nails have changed as much as fashions in make-up – not just colours, but shapes and methods. But the most strikingly different of them all was the 1940s' manicure with bare moons. This was when nails were meticulously painted so as to leave the half-moon shape at the bed of the nail by the cuticle free from colour. It is a beautiful look, but it does tend to foreshorten the nail, so looks best on longer oval-shaped nails. This is quite tricky to do yourself!

1. Start as you would a standard manicure – taking care of your hands and cuticles, and shaping the nail into an oval shape.
2. Paint your nails with a base coat as normal.
3. Using a red, if you wish to be traditional, paint your nails in the normal way, but trying as best as you can not to paint onto the half-moons at all. You can try to achieve the shape now, but don't worry if it looks a bit messy at this point!
4. Do a second coat of colour in the same method.
5. Then take a fine-pointed make-up brush (such as an eyeliner brush), dip it in some nail polish remover and, using this, you can tidy up any bits of colour that have strayed onto the moons and neaten up the arch shape. But take care to wipe the brush every time you use it, or you will end up with streaky moons!
6. When you are happy with all the shapes, add your top coat.

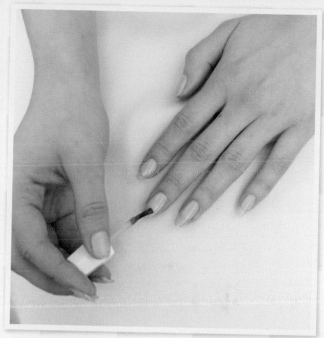

If you find this very difficult, you can try using the arch-shaped stickers you find in French manicure kits – just use them at the base instead of the tips. If you go down this route, make sure you wait until the polish is completely dry before you remove the stickers, so as not to smudge them.

Glossary

Blending brush – thick and round with a soft, angled top.

Blotting papers – small fine tissues for blotting shiny patches.

Blusher brush – smaller round, dome-shaped or softly tapered brush.

Defining brush – very short and very dense, round and pointed.

Eyebrow brush – stiff, very small, flat, straight-edged, angled brush.

Eyeliner – for flicks, liquid, gel or cream liner works best (liquid is wettest, so some people find cream or gel easier to use). For smudgey or smokey looks a soft Kohl pencil is best.

Eyeliner brush – very thin and pointed.

Eyeshadow brush – short, flat, curved top and fluffy.

Hoof stick – angled soft rubber end for pushing back cuticles.

Powder brush – large round, dome-shaped brush.

Retractable lip brush – pointed brush that retracts into itself, with a lid.

Smudger – tapered foam end for softening eyeliner.

Socket brush – soft, slim, long and tapered.

Picture credits

18: Hulton Archive/Archive Photos/Getty Images; 19: Jim Spellman/WireImage/Getty Images; 26: Bettmann/Corbis; 27: Jim Spellman/WireImage/Getty Images; 34: Sunset Boulevard/Corbis; 35: Rune Hellestad/Corbis; 42: Alfred Eisenstaedt/Time & Life Pictures; 43: Charley Gallay/Getty Images Entertainment/Getty Images; 59t: Paramount Pictures/Getty Images Entertainment/Getty Images; 59b: Evan Agostini/Getty Images Entertainment/Getty Images; 60: Popperfoto/Popperfoto/Getty Images; 61: Mike Marsland/WireImage/Getty Images; 70: Henry Groskinsky/Time & Life Images/Getty Images; 71: Steve Granitz/WireImage/Getty Images; 78: Fin Costello/Redferns/Getty Images; 79: Ferdaus Shamim/WireImage/Getty Images; 95: Julian Wasser/Getty Images Entertainment

Acknowledgements

Thanks to

The Powderpuff Girls team
Paul & Joe Beauté
Lola
The Balm
T.LeClerc
Mavala
Mum and Dad x